DATE DUE

NOV 25 2006	
JUL 25 2007	

GAYLORD PRINTED IN U.S.A.

CHEMISTRY
experimenting with science

Antonella Meiani

Lerner Publications Company • Minneapolis

First American edition published in 2003 by Lerner Publications Company

Published by arrangement with Istituto Geografico DeAgostini, Novara, Italy

Originally published as *Il Grande Libro degli Esperimenti*

Copyright © 1999 by Istituto Geografico DeAgostini, Novara, Italy

Translated from the Italian by Maureen Spurgeon.
Translation copyright © 2000 by Brown Watson, England.

This book has been adapted from a single-volume work entitled *Il Grande Libro degli Esperimenti,* originally published by Istituto Geografico DeAgostini, Novara, Italy, in 1999. New back matter was developed by Lerner Publications Company.

Lerner Publications Company
A division of Lerner Publishing Group
241 First Avenue North
Minneapolis, MN 55401 U.S.A.

Website address: www.lernerbooks.com

Library of Congress Cataloging-in-Publication Data

Meiani, Antonella.
    [Il Grande libro degli esperimenti. English. Selections]
    Chemistry / by Antonella Meiani ; [translated from the Italian by Maureen Spurgeon]
1st American ed.
        p.   cm. — (Experimenting with science)
    Includes bibliographical references and index.
    Summary: Uses experiments to explore such topics as how heat changes a substance, the purpose of chemical analysis, and how the human stomach digests food.
    ISBN: 0-8225-0087-6 (lib. bdg. : alk. paper)
    1. Chemistry—Experiments—Juvenile literature. [1. Chemistry—Experiments.
2. Experiments.] I. Title. II. Series: Meiani, Antonella. Experimenting with science.
QD38.M4513 2003
540'.78—dc21   2001050503

Manufactured in the United States of America
1 2 3 4 5 6 – JR – 08 07 06 05 04 03

Table of Contents

Chemistry

Does heat change a substance? When do two substances form a compound? Why do nails rust? What is chemical analysis? How does the human stomach digest food? You will find the answers to these and many more questions by doing the experiments in this section, under the following headings:

- Solids, liquids, and gases
- Mixtures, solutions, and compounds
- Chemical reactions
- Analyzing substances
- Chemistry around us

Solids, liquids, and gases

Everything around us is made up of atoms. These are tiny particles of matter that form molecules with other atoms. But what is the difference between liquid, solid, and gaseous substances? The state of matter – liquid, solid, or gas – depends on the movement of its molecules. In solids, the forces that hold the molecules together, called electromagnetic forces, are very strong. The molecules can vibrate, but they cannot change position. In liquids, the molecules can slide past one another, continually changing position, but they stay close together. In gases, the molecules are kept together by a very weak force. They can move in all directions, and there is a lot of space between molecules. (That is why a gas can be compressed.)

The following experiments will show you the effects of heat on molecules and how a substance changes from one state to another.

All the experiments are safe to do, but an adult must be on hand to use some of the tools that are required.

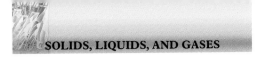

Does heat change a substance?

EXPANSION OF LIQUIDS

You need:
- three identical glass jars with stoppers
- scissors
- three glass tubes, about 20–30 cm (8–12 in.) long
- modeling clay and tape
- water, olive oil, and rubbing alcohol
- rectangular baking dish
- hot plate

What to do:

1 Fill one jar with water, the second with olive oil, and the third with rubbing alcohol. Label the jars with tape.

2 Ask an adult to use the scissors to make a hole in the center of each stopper. Carefully push the glass tubes through. Each should be at the same depth in the jar, but not touching the bottom. Put clay around the top of each tube to hold it firmly.

3 Pour water into the baking dish. Stand the three jars in the water. Ask an adult to put the dish on the hot plate and turn it on.

What happens?
In a little while, the liquid in each of the three jars rises to a different level.

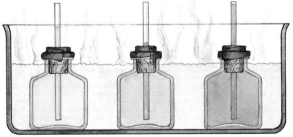

Why?
The heat of the water causes the liquids in the jars to expand (take up more space). (The amount that a liquid expands depends on its density.) There is not enough space inside the jars for the liquids to expand, so they rise up into the glass tubes.

HEAT UP A SOLID

You need:
- coin
- length of steel wire
- clothespin
- lit candle

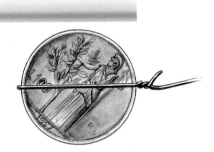

What to do:

1 Make a loop with the wire. It must be the same diameter as the coin so that the loop fits exactly over the coin.

2 Grip the coin with the clothespin. Hold the coin over the flame of the candle for a few minutes.

3 Now try to thread the wire loop over the coin again.

What happens?
The coin no longer passes through.

Why?
The heat of the flame has temporarily made the coin expand. If you let it cool down, you will once more be able to thread it through the loop.

Railway tracks can expand because of excessive heat. That is why there is space between one rail and the next. This space becomes smaller when the rails expand.

Solids, liquids, and gases expand (take up more space) when they are heated.

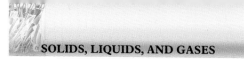
How does matter react to cooling?

AIR THAT SHRINKS

You need:
- glass bottle
- balloon
- sink with hot and cold water

What to do:

1 With the help of an adult, pour very hot water into the bottle.

2 After a few minutes, empty the bottle. Immediately put the neck of the balloon over the top of the bottle.

3 Run cold water over the outside of the bottle.

What happens?
The balloon sinks inside the bottle.

Why?
The hot air inside the bottle contracts (shrinks) when it cools, which means that its volume is reduced. As the air outside enters the bottle and occupies the space that is left, it also pushes the balloon to the inside. The contraction of the air is due to the slowing-down of the speed of its molecules, resulting from the lowering of the temperature.

A special component

Have you ever frozen water to make ice? Then you have seen that ice takes up more space than liquid water. That is why a tightly closed bottle full of water will break if left in the freezer. This expansion of ice is due to the structure of the water molecules. When the temperature falls below 4°C (39°F) these molecules change into bulky hexagonal structures that need more space than liquid water. This is why water leaks can cause trouble during the winter – as water freezes, the ice takes up more space and can split stonework or break roof tiles.

A COLLAPSING BOTTLE

You need:
- ice cubes
- meat tenderizer
- cloth napkin
- plastic bottle with a screw top

What to do:
1 Put some ice cubes in the napkin. Ask an adult to crush the cubes with the meat tenderizer.

2 Put the crushed ice in the bottle. Screw on the top.

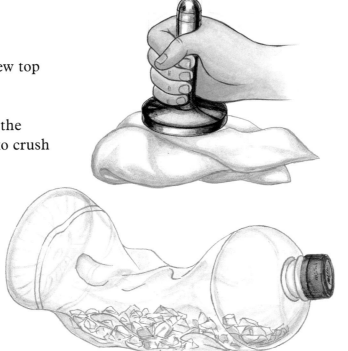

3 Shake the bottle so that the inside is thoroughly chilled. Then put it down.

What happens?
The bottle curls up.

Why?
Inside the bottle, the ice causes a rapid reduction of the air temperature. This means that the air inside is reduced in volume. The air outside presses on the bottle and squashes it.

With the exception of water freezing into ice, when things become cold they contract (become smaller).

Can substances change their physical state?

MOLECULES IN MOVEMENT

You need:
- ice cube
- half a bar of chocolate
- radiator
- hot plate
- saucepan
- two small plates
- water

What to do:

1 Pour a little water in one plate. Place the ice cube in the other plate.

2 Place the two plates on the radiator.

3 Put the chocolate in the saucepan. With the help of an adult, heat it gently on the hot plate.

What happens?

In a short time, the ice changes into water. After a few hours, all of the water disappears. In the saucepan, the chocolate melts and changes into a thick liquid.

Why?

The heat of the radiator makes the water evaporate. This means that the molecules increase their speed, spreading away from each other and dispersing among the air molecules in the form of water vapor. The heat of the radiator also transforms the ice, which is water in its solid state. In the same way, the heat of the hot plate makes the chocolate change from its solid state to liquid.

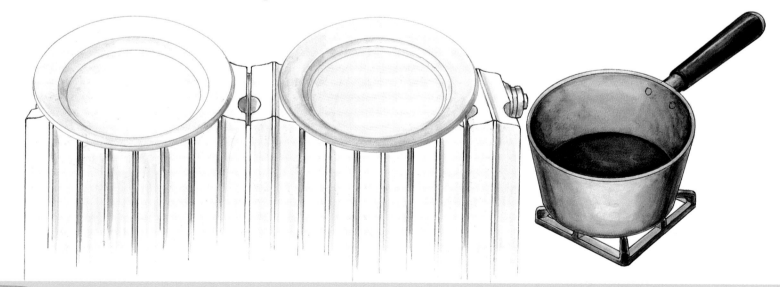

Changes of state

MELTING

FREEZING

PRECIPITATION

SUBLIMATION

CONDENSATION

BOILING/EVAPORATION

The change from the liquid state to the gas (or vapor) state is due to an increase in temperature. In boiling, this happens rapidly and involves the whole mass of liquid. Evaporation, on the other hand, is a slow process that affects only the surface layer of the liquid.

Water vapor is a gas. When it meets a cold surface, it forms tiny drops. (This process is called condensation.) But all gases can be changed into liquids if they are cooled enough (air becomes liquid at minus 195°C [−319°F]) or compressed enough (a spray can contains pressurized gaseous substances in a liquid state).

The melting of ice happens at room temperature, and water freezes below 0°C (32°F). When a volcano erupts, it expels lava, solid rock that has become liquid due to an extraordinarily high temperature. As it cools, the lava returns to its solid state.

Dry ice is carbon dioxide in its solid state. When dry ice comes in contact with air or water, these substances help it to pass directly into a gaseous state (sublimation). The reverse process, from vapor to solid, is called precipitation. Frost forms on very cold days, when water vapor in the air precipitates.

The effects of pressure

Pressure also influences the change of a substance from one state to another. When pressure is increased, this makes the molecules stay close to each other. In a pressure cooker, the steam that is created inside pushes on the surface of the water. As a result, the water reaches the boiling point at a higher temperature (because it needs more heat to overcome the resistance of pressure) and the food gets cooked more quickly.

Variations in temperature or pressure can cause a substance to change from one physical state to another.

Mixtures, solutions, and compounds

Scientists have identified 115 pure substances that are called elements. Each element is made up of the same kind of atom – which means there are 115 different types of atoms.

Atoms combine together to form molecules. The combinations are endless and create an enormous number of substances that make up the whole Universe. But does mixing two elements always produce a new substance? What is the difference between a mixture, like a solution of water and salt, and a chemical compound, like rust?

Do substances change in mixtures?

UNION AND SEPARATION

You need:
- fine salt
- white flour
- spoon
- blotting paper
- funnel
- pitcher
- large see-through container
- water

What to do:

1 In the pitcher, mix together equal amounts of fine salt and white flour.

What happens?
In the mixture, the two substances, flour and salt, cannot be distinguished from one another.

2 Pour water into the pitcher. Mix again. Then wait a little while.

What happens?
After a few minutes, the flour settles on the bottom of the pitcher.

3 Fold the blotting paper into quarters. Hold three of the corners together. Pull the fourth corner away from the others, to make a filter. Now put the base of the filter in the funnel.

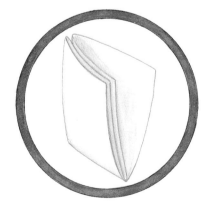

4 Hold the funnel over the large see-through container. Slowly pour the liquid from the pitcher into the filter.

5 Take the filter out of the funnel. Let the filter dry.

6 Put the container with the filtered water in a warm place. Wait until the water evaporates.

What happens?
Flour has collected on the filter. In the container, when all the water has evaporated, there remains a thin layer of salt crystals.

Why?
Flour does not dissolve in water. Instead, it tends to separate from it and settles on the bottom. This phenomenon is called decantation. The particles of flour are too big to pass through the blotting paper, so they stay on the filter. This way of separating a solid substance from a liquid is called filtration. The salt dissolves in the water. It remains dissolved until the heat makes the water evaporate. Then the salt returns to its solid state in the form of crystals. This method of separating the components of a solution is called crystallization.

Substances that form a mixture do not change and can be easily separated.

Chemical reactions

In chemical reactions, the elements or compounds we begin with are called *reactants* (which means they can undergo a reaction), and the end results are called *products*. There are chemical reactions of *synthesis* in which the reactants combine to create a new compound, and there are chemical reactions of *analysis* in which the reactants divide into the elements that they are made of. There are also reactions of *substitution* in which one or more elements of the reactants change partners. By doing the following experiments, you can try different types of chemical reactions with air, heat, and electricity.

Why do nails rust?

IRON OXIDIZES

You need:
- iron filings
- test tube
- see-through bowl
- pen that can write on glass
- water

What to do:

1 Dampen the inside of the test tube. Then shake in a few iron filings so that they stick to the sides of the tube.

2 Pour about 3 cm (1 in.) of cold water into the bowl.

3 Turn the test tube upside-down and stand it on the bottom of the bowl. The level of water inside the test tube should be level with the water in the bowl. (To do this, slightly tip the test tube as you place it in the water.)

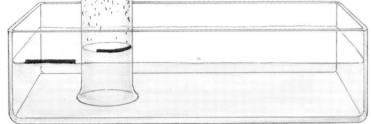

4 Use the pen to mark the level of the water, both on the test tube and on the bowl. Then set the experiment aside for two days.

What happens?
The iron filings have turned brown. The level of water in the test tube has risen. The level of water in the bowl has gone down.

Why?
The iron combined with the oxygen in the air inside the test tube to form rust. The chemical name for rust is iron oxide. In this chemical reaction, which we call oxidation, the oxygen has left the air and combined with the iron. This means that the volume of air inside the test tube has decreased. The air outside has pressed down on the surface of the water in the bowl, pushing it up inside the test tube so that it fills the space left by the oxygen.

Oxidation reactions

The rust that forms on iron objects corrodes (eats into) those objects, making them weaker. Once rust has formed, it remains on the object, making the outer layers crumble and exposing the inner layers of metal to the air. These layers in turn also become oxidized, forming more rust. Another example of oxidation is when slices of apple turn brown, because a substance in the apple combines with the oxygen in the air. The blackening of objects made of silver is also an oxidation reaction.

Mars is distinguished from other heavenly bodies by its red color. This is due to the oxidation of iron on its surface.

When iron is oxidized, oxygen bonds with the iron, creating a new substance—iron oxide, or rust.

Do chemical reactions change compounds?

A LITTLE BANG

You need:
- iron filings
- copper sulfate
- two test tubes
- hot water
- vinegar
- match

What to do:

1 Pour some hot water into one test tube. Add a small amount of copper sulfate. Shake the test tube to mix the two substances.

2 Put some iron filings in the other test tube. Then fill it halfway with vinegar. Carefully put two drops of this solution into the first test tube.

3 When you see bubbles forming, cover the test tube with your thumb.

4 Ask an adult to strike a match and hold it near the mouth of the test tube.

5 When you feel the pressure of gas inside the test tube, remove your thumb.

What happens?
The flame makes a little bang.

Why?
One of the components of vinegar is hydrogen. When the vinegar reacts with iron and copper sulfate, hydrogen gas is released. When the hydrogen escapes from the test tube, the match makes it burst into flame with a little bang.

A GAS SET FREE

You need:
- sodium bicarbonate (baking soda)
- teaspoon
- vinegar
- water
- a tall, straight glass
- match

What to do:

1 Pour a finger's width of water into the glass.

2 Add a teaspoon of sodium bicarbonate and a little vinegar.

3 Ask an adult to light a match and hold it down inside the glass.

What happens?
The flame goes out.

Why?
The sodium bicarbonate is a compound of sodium, hydrogen, carbon, and oxygen. In the chemical reaction, it breaks up when it comes in contact with the vinegar. The carbon and oxygen separate from the other elements. Together they form a gas, carbon dioxide, that puts out the flame.

CHANGES IN THE ELEMENTS

You need:
- test tube
- water
- copper sulfate
- iron filings

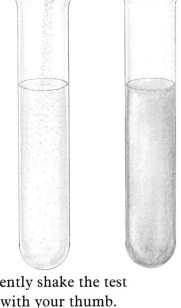

What to do:

1 Fill two thirds of the test tube with water.

2 Add some copper sulfate.

What happens?
You get a blue solution.

3 Add the iron filings. Gently shake the test tube, holding it closed with your thumb.

What happens?
A red substance settles on the bottom of the test tube. The solution becomes clear green.

Why?
The copper sulfate contains copper. When you add the iron filings, the iron and the copper change places. The iron bonds to the sulfur, forming iron sulfate, which gives the solution a green color. The copper settles at the bottom of the test tube.

Chemical reactions can separate, combine, or rearrange elements.

Is combustion a chemical reaction?

A CANDLE DOES NOT ONLY GIVE LIGHT

You need:
- candle
- candleholder
- match
- knife
- microscope slide
- clothespin

What to do:

1 Put the candle in the candleholder. Ask an adult to light it.

2 Hold the blade of the knife at the center of the flame for a few seconds.

What happens?
The blade is covered with soot, which is tiny particles of the element carbon.

Why?
These particles are found in the central part of the flame. They are caused by the breakdown of the paraffin (wax) of which the candle is made.

3 Using the clothespin, hold the microscope slide in the flame, at the very tip of the wick, for about 10–15 seconds. Then allow the slide to cool.

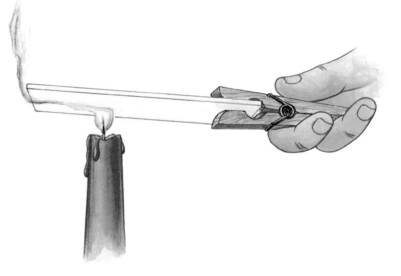

What happens?
There are traces of wax on the slide.

Why?
Not all of the wax breaks down when the flame burns. Some bits of melted wax are drawn up by the rising heat. On contact with the surface of the slide, the wax becomes solid again.

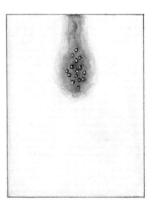

When a candle burns

The body of a candle is made of solid paraffin, which is made of hydrogen and carbon, and a paraffin-soaked wick. The flame that begins when the wick is lit is not the same throughout. The outermost zone of the flame is in contact with the oxygen in the air, so that is where the burning of the paraffin begins. This gives off heat. In the central zone of the flame, there is no oxygen. There the paraffin molecules break down into hydrogen and carbon. The heat makes the carbon become incandescent (glowing), which makes the flame bright.

The heat produced by combustion melts some of the wax, which drips down the sides of the candle and then solidifies again.

Fire

Combustion is a chemical reaction that is often accompanied by a flame. A combustible material (for example, the sulfur of a match) combines with a combustive agent (such as oxygen) to produce heat. Combustion usually happens when a flame or a spark is used to light a combustible substance. Heat is produced, and this adds to the combustion.

The vital elements of combustion are the combustible material, the combustive agent, and heat. When any of these three elements is missing, the fire will go out.

Smoke, cinders, and soot are all products showing that a chemical transformation takes place when something burns.

COMBUSTIVE AGENT

HEAT

COMBUSTIBLE MATERIAL

Combustion is a chemical reaction. When a substance burns, it changes and produces new substances.

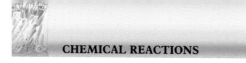
Can electricity cause a chemical reaction?

DISAPPEARING WATER

You need:
- 4.5-volt battery
- two pieces of electrical cable, with the plastic stripped off the ends (ask an adult to do this for you)
- wire
- lead for a mechanical pencil
- tape
- two test tubes
- vinegar
- water
- see-through glass container
- two clothespins
- matches

What to do:

1 Break the pencil lead in two. Wind one end of a wire around each of the battery contacts. Wind the free end of each wire around a piece of lead and tape firmly, as shown in the picture. You have made two electrodes.

2 Fill the container with water. Put in the two electrodes so that they touch the bottom. Attach the electric cables to the edges of the container with the two clothespins.

3 Fill one test tube with water, and hold your finger over the top. Turn the tube upside-down in the container. Take away your finger and put the tube over the top of one electrode. Do the same with the other test tube and the second electrode.

4 Pour some vinegar into the container. Then wait a few hours.

What happens?
Bubbles have formed in the test tubes. After a few hours, the level of water inside the test tubes has dropped.

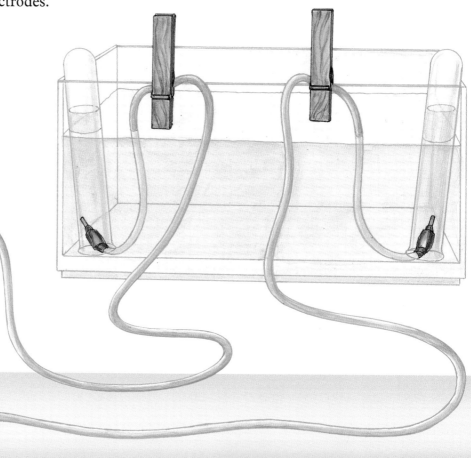

5 Disconnect the wire ends from the battery.

6 Take the test tube with the lowest level of water out of the container, keeping your thumb over the top.

7 Turn the test tube the right way up. Ask an adult to hold a lit match near the mouth of the tube, then take away your thumb.

What happens?
There is a little bang.

8 Now take the other test tube from the container in the same way. Ask an adult to light a match and put it out, then put it into the test tube as soon as you take your thumb away.

What happens?
The match bursts into flame again.

Why?
The electricity provided by the battery has caused a chemical reaction that separated the components of water, hydrogen and oxygen. This process is called electrolysis. It is also used to separate compounds that are dissolved in water. The first test tube contains hydrogen, which explodes with the heat of the flame. The second test tube contains oxygen, which is able to make the match burn again.

Chemical reactions can generate electricity

Inside the batteries that we use to power toys and electrical equipment is a chemical substance called ammonium chloride paste. When the metal cap of the battery touches the metal tabs in a toy's battery compartment, a chemical reaction begins inside the battery. This reaction generates electricity. Little by little, as the current is produced, the ammonium chloride paste is used up, and the battery is finally exhausted.

Electrical current can break up water, as well as the substances dissolved in it.

Do chemical reactions produce heat?

HEAT FROM NOTHING

You need:
- plaster powder
- water
- deep plastic tray
- spoon

What to do:

1 Empty the plaster powder into the tray. Add water according to the directions on the package and mix with the plaster to make a stiff, thick paste.

2 Leave the paste for about an hour.

What happens?
The plaster hardens and the sides of the plastic tray become hot.

Why?
The hardening of the plaster is due to the chemical reaction of the plaster powder with the water. One of the products of this reaction is heat.

The conservation of matter

French chemist Antoine Lavoisier lived in the eighteenth century. He was the first to understand that matter is neither created nor destroyed in chemical reactions, but undergoes transformation. He demonstrated that the total mass of the original substances is equal to the total mass of compounds that are produced, and the number of atoms present does not change during the reaction. Instead, the atoms change their arrangement and the atomic bonds by which they are connected. Today it is accepted that the principle of conservation of mass (or the Lavoisier principle) does not apply to nuclear reactions, in which some matter is destroyed and transformed into energy.

A portrait of Lavoiser (left) and a reconstruction of his scientific laboratory (above).

HEAT RETURNS

You need:
- copper sulfate crystals
- test tube
- water
- hot plate
- eyedropper
- piece of paper

What to do:

1 Fold the paper into a thick strip to make a test tube holder.

2 Put some copper sulfate crystals into the test tube. Ask an adult to use the paper holder to carefully hold it over the hot plate.

What happens?
The crystals turn white. Drops of water form in the upper part of the test tube.

3 Let the test tube cool. Use the eyedropper to add two drops of water.

What happens?
The crystals turn blue and the test tube heats up.

Why?
The copper sulfate crystals contain molecules of water. With the addition of heat, water molecules evaporate and make the crystals lose their blue color. When you add water, the water molecules return to the crystals. This chemical reaction, reversing the previous reaction, produces the same amount of heat that was absorbed before.

Copper sulfate crystals

During some chemical reactions, energy contained in the reactants is released in the form of heat.

Analyzing substances

Some characteristics of substances that we come into contact with each day are immediately recognizable by our senses. Taste, smell, color, and consistency of materials or foods enable us to distinguish, classify, use, or avoid them. In some cases, however, we cannot recognize characteristics by our senses. Although some people may try to find out about substances by tasting or touching them, this can often be very dangerous. There are many safe methods to discover the chemical nature of substances. In these pages, we will learn about some simple ones.

Can we discover the presence of one substance in another?

AIR IN AIR

You need:
- limewater (obtainable from a pharmacy or a shop that stocks chemical products)
- drinking straw
- a glass
- bicycle pump

What to do:

1 Pour the limewater into the glass.

2 Put the tube of the bicycle pump into the glass. Pump in a little air.

3 Now put the straw into the glass. Blow into the water.

What happens?
When the pump blows air into the water, bubbles form, but the limewater remains clear. When you blow into the water, however, it becomes cloudy.

Why?
The limewater becomes cloudy when it comes into contact with carbon dioxide gas. This shows that carbon dioxide is present in the air that we breathe out, but not in the air that comes from the bicycle pump. In the process of breathing, we inhale mostly nitrogen and oxygen, but we breathe out mostly carbon dioxide.

WHERE IS THE STARCH?

You need:
- samples of bread, rice, pasta, meat, apple, potato, and white flour
- tincture of iodine
- water
- a glass
- eyedropper
- starch powder
- seven small plates

What to do:

1 Fill the glass one-third full of water. Add six drops of iodine.

2 With the eyedropper, put a few drops of this solution on some starch powder.

What happens?
The starch turns blue.

3 Set out each food sample on a plate. Dampen each one with water. Using the eyedropper, add a few drops of the water and iodine solution to each.

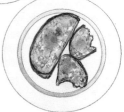

What happens?
Some of the food has turned blue where you added the iodine solution.

Why?
The blue color is the sign that there is starch in some of the foods. Starch is a compound that is very common in vegetables. Plants make starch and store it in their seeds and roots. The iodine solution turns blue in the presence of starch.

Some substances change color when they come into contact with certain other substances.

What is the purpose of chemical analysis?

CORROSIVE VINEGAR

You need:
- an eggshell
- flakes of wall plaster
- vinegar
- two glasses

What to do:

1 Put the eggshell into one glass. Put the flakes of plaster into the other glass.

2 Fill each glass half full with vinegar. Check the contents every 12 hours for a few days.

What happens?
First the eggshell, and then the flakes of wall plaster, dissolve in the vinegar.

Why?
In chemistry, vinegar is a substance that is defined as an acid. This means it is able to corrode (eat away at) some substances, such as calcium, which is a component of both the eggshell and the plaster.

Acid substances and base substances

Acids and bases are two important types of chemical substances. Determining whether a substance is an acid or a base is the first thing to do in order to find out the composition of a substance and how it will react with other substances.
Some acids have a sour taste (such as lemons and vinegar) and are virtually harmless. More powerful acids are dangerous and can burn skin on contact. Bases are substances that are often present in detergents, but strong bases can be dangerous because they are corrosive. When a base can be dissolved in water it is called an alkali.

Pure water is neither an acid nor a base; it is neutral. The pH scale is used to indicate how acidic or basic a substance is. A pH of 7 indicates a neutral substance, such as pure water. Acids have a pH value lower than 7, and the lower the pH, the stronger the acid. Bases have a pH value higher than 7, and the greater the pH, the stronger the base. Even in the human body there are substances with different pH levels. Gastric (stomach) juices have a pH lower than 3, and blood has a pH a little higher than 7.

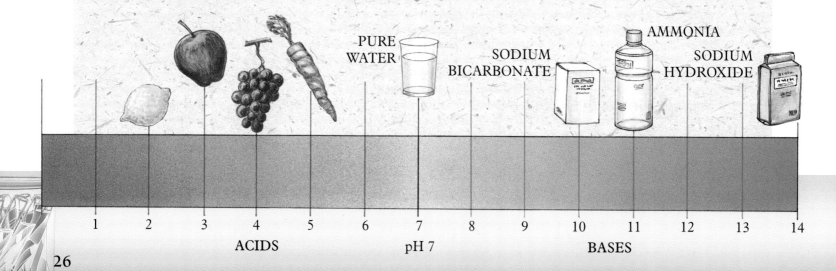

PURE WATER

SODIUM BICARBONATE

AMMONIA

SODIUM HYDROXIDE

| 1 | 2 | 3 | 4 | 5 | 6 | 7 | 8 | 9 | 10 | 11 | 12 | 13 | 14 |

ACIDS   pH 7   BASES

A LIQUID INDICATOR

You need:

- half a red cabbage
- knife
- saucepan
- hot plate
- water
- strainer
- glass jar
- three glasses
- lemon juice
- sodium bicarbonate
- spoon

What to do:

1 Ask an adult to cut the red cabbage into thin slices. Put the slices in the saucepan and cover with water. Place on the hot plate to cook.

2 When the water begins to boil, stir the cabbage, then turn off the heat and leave for half an hour.

3 Put the strainer on the jar. Pour the cabbage into the strainer so that the water filters through into the jar. You now have a liquid indicator.

4 Pour some water and some lemon juice into a glass. Pour water with sodium bicarbonate into another glass. Put plain water in the third glass.

5 Add a spoonful of the liquid indicator to each glass.

What happens?

The water with the lemon juice turns red. The water with sodium bicarbonate turns blue-green. The plain water is just slightly tinged with the same color as the liquid indicator.

Why?

The liquid that you obtained by boiling the red cabbage is an indicator, a substance that has a special ability to take on a different color depending on whether it comes into contact with an acid or an alkali.

In this experiment, the liquid indicator turned red to show you that lemon juice is an acid substance, and blue-green to show that sodium bicarbonate is an alkali substance. The water is neither acid nor base, so it did not make the indicator change color.

The international symbol for acid substances (right)

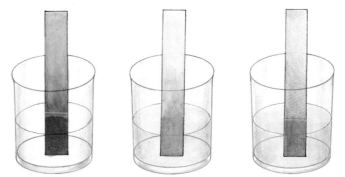

Different indicators are used in chemical laboratories. Among them are litmus papers—strips of paper soaked in a special substance that changes color when it comes into contact with an acid or an alkali—and methyl orange, which reveals the presence of an alkali by turning pink.

Indicators used in chemical analysis of substances reveal characteristics that are not immediately obvious.

Chemistry around us

Many chemical reactions happen all around us. Chemistry happens every time we cook an egg or bake a cake, when we breathe, when we chew, and when we digest our food.

In these pages, you will find some simple experiments that will give you some idea about what happens to food when it is being prepared and when it is eaten.

How does yeast make dough rise?

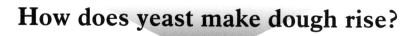

THE FORCE OF BUBBLES

You need:
- plastic bottle
- about 150 ml (5 oz.) of warm water
- yeast
- sugar
- teaspoon
- balloon

What to do:

1 Put three teaspoons of yeast into the bottle. Add two teaspoons of sugar.

2 Slowly fill the bottle halfway with warm water.

3 Place the balloon on the neck of the bottle. Wait about one hour.

What happens?
The liquid becomes frothy and the balloon inflates.

Why?
Yeast is a microscopic fungus that feeds on the natural sugar contained in flour. As this happens, a gas – carbon dioxide – is produced. This gas forms lots of bubbles that rise to the surface. (That is why the liquid becomes frothy.) The gas expands into the air above, inflating the balloon.

The rising of dough

In bread making, the yeast feeds on the starch contained in flour and produces carbon dioxide that makes the dough rise. During baking, the dough solidifies around the bubbles of carbon dioxide, forming the little holes that we see in bread.

Chemical substances in foods

The foods that we eat are generally formed of natural chemical substances that we get from plants and from animals.

The substances that we must eat to stay healthy can be subdivided into three groups:

- carbohydrates (found in pasta, bread, sugar, fruit, and green vegetables) give us immediate energy because they are burned up quickly by our bodies.
- fats (such as cooking oil, butter, and margarine) also give us energy, but at a slower rate.
- proteins (found in meat, fish, eggs, and cheese) are needed for growth, healthy bones, and the maintenance of the body.

Foods also provide us with other important substances – vitamins, minerals, and some of the water that we need every day.

As yeast converts the starch contained in flour, it gives off a gas called carbon dioxide, which makes dough rise.

How does the stomach break up food?

ENZYMES AT WORK

You need:
- two glass jars
- two hard-boiled eggs (with shells removed)
- ordinary detergent
- biological detergent with enzymes
- warm water
- spoon
- pen
- two labels

What to do:

1 Put a spoonful of ordinary detergent in one jar. Put a spoonful of biological detergent with enzymes in the other jar.

2 Label the jars to show which is which.

3 Pour water in both jars. Mix thoroughly until the detergent is dissolved.

4 Put a hard-boiled egg in each jar. Place the jars in a warm place, but not in direct contact with a source of heat. Leave for a few days.

Biochemistry

Inside the human body, as in all living organisms, countless chemical reactions take place. The study of these phenomena is the science of biochemistry. Biochemists carry out research to discover how molecules of inanimate (nonliving) substances react together to keep organisms (living things) alive.

Biochemistry is very important in the field of medicine. Studies of bodily functions (such as breathing, digestion, and the transmission of nerve impulses) have made it possible to develop new medicines for many diseases and afflictions.

The food industry has also used the knowledge gained by biochemistry, especially in the preservation of foods and the manufacture of foods for babies.

What happens?
In the jar with the ordinary detergent, the egg has not changed. In the jar with the biological detergent, the egg looks partly eaten.

Why?
The biological detergent contains enzymes. An enzyme is a special chemical substance that either makes a chemical reaction possible or speeds up a chemical reaction. The enzymes in the biological detergent "eat" at the egg the same way that they do with a speck of dirt, by separating the molecules and making them dissolve in water. Our body produces enzymes to break up food into very small particles that the digestive system can use more easily.

THE ACTION OF SALIVA

You need:
- iodine solution (as made for the experiment to detect starch)
- white flour
- cold water, lukewarm water, and hot water
- spoon
- teaspoon
- cup
- test tube
- glass jar
- eyedropper
- plate

What to do:

1 In the cup, mix a spoonful of flour with a little cold water. Then fill the cup with hot water.

2 Let the mixture cool. Then spoon a little onto a plate. Add one or two drops of the iodine solution.

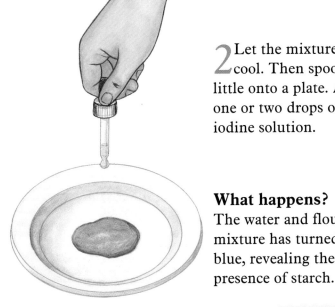

What happens?
The water and flour mixture has turned blue, revealing the presence of starch.

3 Put as much saliva (spit) as you can into a test tube. Add a spoonful of the water and flour mixture. Shake vigorously, holding your thumb over the top of the test tube.

4 Pour some lukewarm water into the jar. Then put the test tube in the jar. (Do not let any water get inside the test tube.)

5 Every half hour, remove a little of the contents of the test tube with the eyedropper and repeat the test with the iodine solution. Remember to wash the plate after each test.

What happens?
As time passes, the iodine solution causes less of a color change in the flour mixture. Eventually, adding the iodine solution produces no blue color at all.

Why?
Saliva contains an enzyme (amylase) that is able to transform the starch into maltose, a sugar that is more easily digested by the body. Try to chew a little piece of bread very slowly. It tastes salty at first, then sweet. That change happens because of the action of the amylase.

Our bodies produce enzymes that transform foods into substances that are easier to digest.

What are mixtures?

Mixtures are made by combining substances that keep their characteristics (they do not change) and are easily separated. Sometimes these substances can be recognized by the naked eye. At other times, the components of a mixture can be seen only with a special microscope.

The components of a mixture may be solids, liquids, or gases.

Here are a few examples of mixtures:

solid with solid
- Metal alloys, such as bronze (copper and tin) and brass (copper and zinc), are mixtures made by melting the metals together at high temperatures and then letting them solidify.
- Sand is a mixture of grains of different minerals.

solid with liquid
- The water that soaks into the sand during a sea storm is a mixture.

solid with gas
- The smoke of a candle is a mixture of air and microscopic particles produced by the wax as it burns.

liquid with liquid
- Oil can be combined with water to form a mixture called an emulsion. These two liquids never mix perfectly together.
- Milk is an emulsion of water and fat.

liquid with gas
- Mist is tiny droplets of water mixed with the air.

Metals and nonmetals

Natural chemical elements can be grouped into categories according to the characteristics that they show. An important subdivision distinguishes metals from nonmetals. Metals are mostly solid at room temperature, except for mercury, which is a liquid. Most metals have a shiny color similar to silver, although copper is red, and gold is yellow. All metals are good conductors of both electrical current and heat. They are easy to work with; they are ductile (they can be drawn out into a thin wire) and malleable (they can be pounded into thin sheets). Other examples of metals are iron, aluminum, and uranium.

Nonmetals have a wider range of characteristics. They may be gases, like oxygen, nitrogen, and helium; or solids, such as sulfur and carbon. Nonmetals are not shiny like metals, and they do not conduct electricity or heat. They are fragile and are not as ductile or malleable as metals.

Metric Conversion Table

When you know:	Multiply by:	To find:
inches (in.)	2.54	centimeters (cm)
feet (ft.)	0.3048	meters (m)
yards (yd.)	0.9144	meters (m)
miles (mi.)	1.609	kilometers (km)
square feet (sq. ft.)	0.093	square meters (m^2)
square miles (sq. mi.)	2.59	square kilometers (km^2)
acres	0.405	hectares (ha)
quarts (qt.)	0.946	liters (l)
gallons (gal.)	3.785	liters (l)
ounces (oz.)	28.35	grams (g)
pounds (lb.)	0.454	kilograms (kg)
tons	0.907	metric tons (t)

To convert degrees Fahrenheit (°F) to degrees Celsius (°C), subtract 32, then multiply by $\frac{5}{9}$.

Glossary

acids: chemical compounds containing hydrogen that react with bases to form salts. Acids turn blue litmus paper red. Strong acids can burn skin.

alkalis: bases that dissolve in water

alloys: mixtures of two or more metals

analysis reactions: chemical reactions in which compounds are broken down into the elements that they are made of

atoms: the smallest parts of a chemical element that have all the properties of that element

bases: substances that react with acids to form salts. Bases turn red litmus paper blue. Strong bases can burn skin.

biochemistry: the science that studies the chemistry of plant and animal life

carbohydrates: substances such as sugars and starches that are made up of carbon, hydrogen, and oxygen. Carbohydrates provide a quick source of energy. Foods such as bread, rice, potatoes, and pasta are good sources of carbohydrates.

chemistry: the scientific study of substances, what they are composed of, and the ways in which they react with each other

combustible: capable of burning

combustion: a chemical reaction in which oxygen and fuel combine to produce heat and often a flame

compounds: chemical substances formed by combining two or more elements. A compound's properties are different from the properties of the elements of which it is made.

compress: to press or squeeze something so that it takes up less space

condensation: the act of changing from a gas to a liquid

conservation of mass: in a chemical reaction, the total mass of the original substances is equal to the total mass of the products

contract: to become smaller

corrode: to gradually destroy or eat away at something. Rust corrodes objects made of iron or steel.

crystallization: a method of separating a compound out of a liquid solution by changing the compound into its solid state in the form of crystals

decantation: a method of separating a compound from a liquid in which it is suspended. The mixture is allowed to sit undisturbed so that the compound settles to the bottom of the container.

digest: to change food in the stomach and intestines into a form that can be used by the body

ductile: able to be drawn out into a thin wire

electrolysis: breaking a dissolved chemical compound into its parts by passing an electric current through it

electromagnetic forces: the forces that hold molecules together

elements: substances that cannot be broken down into simpler substances

emulsions: mixtures of liquids, such as oil and water, in which very fine drops of one stay evenly scattered throughout the other. Milk and mayonnaise are emulsions.

enzymes: chemical substances that cause chemical reactions to occur or that speed up chemical reactions

evaporation: the act of changing from a liquid to a gas

expand: to become larger

fats: oily substances found in the bodies of animals and in some plants. Fats provide the body with energy. Fats are found in foods such as meat, milk, nuts, and avocados.

filtration: a method of separating a compound from a liquid in which it is suspended. The mixture is poured into a funnel lined with thick paper through which the liquid can pass but the compound cannot.

freezing: the act of changing from a liquid to a solid

gases: substances that spread out to fill any space available. Air is a mixture of gases.

inanimate: without life

incandescent: glowing

indicators: substances that change color when they come in contact with certain other substances. Iodine is an indicator that turns blue when it comes in contact with starch molecules.

limewater: a water solution of calcium hydroxide, an alkali. Limewater is used as an antacid.

liquids: substances that flow easily. Water is a liquid at room temperature.

litmus paper: paper soaked in a dye that indicates whether a solution is acidic or basic. An acid makes blue litmus paper turn red, and a base makes red litmus paper turn blue.

malleable: able to be pounded into a thin sheet

melting: the act of changing from a solid to a liquid

metals: chemical elements that conduct heat and electricity, can be hammered or stretched, and are usually shiny. Iron, gold, aluminum, lead, and magnesium are metals.

mixtures: two or more elements or compounds mixed together but not united chemically

molecules: the smallest parts of a substance that have all the properties of that substance. A molecule is made up of one or more atoms.

nonmetals: chemical elements that do not conduct heat or electricity, are not shiny, and are often breakable

organisms: living things

oxidation reactions: chemical reactions in which a chemical element or compound combines with oxygen

oxides: compounds made of oxygen and one or more other chemical elements. Rust, or iron oxide, is made of oxygen and iron.

pH: a measure of how acidic or basic a substance is

precipitation: the act of changing from a gas to a solid

products: the end results of a chemical reaction

proteins: substances containing nitrogen and other elements. Proteins are found in all living things and are needed for growth, healthy bones, and the maintenance of the body. Foods such as meat, cheese, eggs, and beans are good sources of protein.

reactants: the atoms or molecules that combine in a chemical reaction

reactions: changes caused by chemical action

solids: substances that keep their shape instead of flowing or spreading out

solutions: mixtures made by dissolving a substance in a liquid

sublimation: the act of changing from a solid to a gas

substances: things that have weight and take up space; also called matter

substitution reactions: chemical reactions in which atoms or groups of atoms switch places with one another

synthesis reactions: chemical reactions in which atoms or compounds combine to form a new compound

vapor: a substance in its gaseous state

For Further Reading

Asimov, Isaac. *Asimov's Chronology of Science and Discovery.* New York: HarperCollins, 1994.

Fleisher, Paul. *Liquids and Gases: Principles of Fluid Mechanics.* Minneapolis: Lerner Publications Company, 2002.

_____. *Matter and Energy.* Minneapolis: Lerner Publications Company, 2002.

Gold-Dworkin, Heidi, and Robert K. Ullman. *Fun with Mixing and Chemistry.* New York: McGraw-Hill Professional Publishing, 2000.

Mebane, Robert C., and Thomas R. Rybolt. *Adventures with Atoms and Molecules: Chemistry Experiments for Young People.* Berkeley Heights, NJ: Enslow Publishers, Inc., 1998.

Moje, Steven W. *Cool Chemistry: Great Experiments with Simple Stuff.* New York: Sterling Publications, 1999.

Richards, Jon. *Chemicals & Reactions.* Brookfield, CT: Millbrook Press, 2000.

Vancleave, Janice Pratt. *Janice Vancleave's Chemistry for Every Kid: 101 Easy Experiments that Really Work.* New York: John Wiley & Sons, 1989.

Wood, Robert W. *Who?: Famous Experiments for the Young Scientist.* Philadelphia: Chelsea House Publishers, 1999.

Websites

Cool Science, sponsored by the U.S. Department of Energy
<http://www.fetc.doe.gov/coolscience/index.html>

The Franklin Institute Science Museum online
<http://www.fi.edu/tfi/welcome.html>

NPR's *Sounds Like Science* site
<http://www.npr.org/programs/science>

PBS's *A Science Odyssey* site
<http://www.pbs.org/wgbh/aso>

Science Learning Network
<http://www.sln.org>

Science Museum of Minnesota
<http://www.smm.org>

Index

Photo Acknowledgments

The photographs in this book are reproduced by permission of: Fotoservice/Filser, W. 5; Vergani, A., 6, 12–13; Pozzoni, C., 7; Sappa, C., 9; Buss, W., 14; Cigolini, G., 15a, 23, 24; Dagli Orti G., 22a; Ciccione, 22b; Chasseria, N., 30. Front cover (top): Corbis Royalty Free Images; front cover (bottom): Todd Strand/Independent Picture Service; back cover (bottom): © Pallava Bagla/CORBIS.

Illustrations by Pier Giorgio Citterio.

About the Author

Antonella Meiani is an elementary schoolteacher in Milan, Italy. She has written several books and has worked as a consultant for many publishing houses. With this series, she hopes to offer readers the opportunity to have fun with science, to satisfy their curiosity, and to learn essential concepts through the simple joy of experimentation.